Alive in the WORD

CONNECTING WITH THE SACRAMENTS

I0792875

BAPTISM

Alive in Christ

Justin Huyck

Little Rock Scripture Study

LITURGICAL PRESS
Collegeville, Minnesota

www.littlerockscripture.org

Nihil obstat: Reverend Robert Harren, J.C.L., *Censor deputatus.*
Imprimatur: ✠ Most Reverend Donald J. Kettler, J.C.L., Bishop of Saint Cloud, August 8, 2019.

Cover design by Ann Blattner. Cover photo: Getty Images

Photos/illustrations: Pages 6, 8, 10, 13, 14, 19, 21, 25, 28, 31, 33, 34, 36, 38, Getty Images. Used with permission.

Printed in the United States of America.

ISBN: 978-0-8146-6403-2 978-0-8146-6429-2 (ebook)

Contents

Introduction

Alive in the Word brings you resources to deepen your understanding of Scripture, offer meaning for your life today, and help you to pray and act in response to God's word.

Use any volume of **Alive in the Word** in the way best suited to you.

- **For individual learning and reflection,** consider this an invitation to prayerfully journal in response to the questions you find along the way. And be prepared to move from head to heart and then to action.
- **For group learning and reflection,** arrange for three sessions where you will use the material provided as the basis for faith sharing and prayer. You may ask group members to read each chapter in advance and come prepared with questions answered. In this kind of session, plan to be together for about an hour. Or, if your group prefers, read and respond to the questions together without advance preparation. With this approach, it's helpful to plan on spending more time for each group session in order to adequately work through each of the chapters.

- **For a parish-wide event or use within a larger group,** provide each person with a copy of this volume, and allow time during the event for quiet reading, group discussion and prayer, and then a final commitment by each person to some simple action in response to what he or she learned.

This volume on the topic of baptism is one of several volumes that explore **Connecting with the Sacraments.** Scripture offers a wealth of ways to reflect on the grace we access in our sacramental lives. By spending time with passages that focus on the spiritual dynamics of each sacrament, our own experiences of the sacraments will deepen. Our ability to appreciate how God works in our lives and in the lives of others will expand.

Alive in God's Love

Begin by quietly asking God to assist you in your prayer and study. Then read the account of the baptism of Jesus from the first chapter of Mark.

Mark 1:4-11
4John [the] Baptist appeared in the desert proclaiming a bap-
tism of repentance for the forgiveness of sins. 5People of the
whole Judean countryside and all the inhabitants of Jerusalem
were going out to him and were being baptized by him in the
Jordan River as they acknowledged their sins. 6John was
clothed in camel's hair, with a leather belt around his waist.
He fed on locusts and wild honey. 7And this is what he pro-
claimed: "One mightier than I is coming after me. I am not
worthy to stoop and loosen the thongs of his sandals. 8I have
baptized you with water; he will baptize you with the holy
Spirit."

9It happened in those days that Jesus came from Nazareth
of Galilee and was baptized in the Jordan by John. 10On com-

ing up out of the water he saw the heavens being torn open and the Spirit, like a dove, descending upon him. [11]And a voice came from the heavens, "You are my beloved Son; with you I am well pleased."

Following a few moments of quiet reflection on the passage from the Gospel of Mark, consider the background information provided in Setting the Scene.

Setting the Scene

What is your understanding of baptism? How would you explain it to someone?

At the heart of our baptismal identity is the knowledge that each one of us is loved by God. We are elements of God's creation and, like the cosmos that flowed from primordial waters, God looks upon his good creation in us and is well pleased (v. 11; see Gen 1:31). As baptized disciples of Christ, the goodness of our baptismal identity is manifest in Christ's own baptism in the Jordan, in which we know God's intimacy with us and through which we also have emerged into the promised land of Christ's life.

In the Gospel of Mark, Jesus' baptism is not simply an account of a past event, a prologue before Mark's rushing and roaring story of Jesus' mighty deeds and authoritative teaching. Rather, in this story we hear an ongoing proclamation of Jesus' core identity: this is Christ, Son of God, anointed with God's love (v. 1; Mark 15:39). As followers of the risen Christ, we too are invited to enter into and tell the story of God's love among us (Mark 16:15).

Mark 1:4-11 will be explored a few verses at a time to deepen your understanding. The questions in the margins may be used for personal reflection or group discussion.

Understanding the Scene Itself

[4]John [the] Baptist appeared in the desert proclaiming a baptism of repentance for the forgiveness of sins. [5]People of the whole Judean countryside and all the inhabitants of Jerusalem were going out to him and were being baptized by him in the Jordan River as they acknowledged their sins. [6]John was clothed in camel's hair, with a leather belt around his waist. He fed on locusts and wild honey.

Why would one enter the desert wilderness, a place of vulnerability, a place apart? The figure of John the Baptist suggests a motivation. He appears in the desert like the Old Testament prophet Elijah—wearing a hairy garment, with a leather belt (v. 6; 2 Kgs 1:8)—proclaiming a baptism of repentance for the forgiveness of sins. In both his unkempt appearance and stark diet, John is a visible exaggeration of what we often recognize but can't quite articulate: something is not right with our normal patterns of living in the world, and we may need

to drastically refocus, even away from ordinary concerns like dining and appearance.

According to the gospel text, "the whole Judean countryside" and "all the inhabitants of Jerusalem"—both rural folk and city-dwellers—streamed into the desert to see John and be baptized by him. Perhaps they discovered what we have found in our day: society tends to squelch the fullness of our identity by separating us from one another. To step into the wilderness is to enter a place of encounter with God, often by embracing what Pope Francis calls the "'mystique' of living together, of mingling and encounter, of embracing and supporting one another, of stepping into this flood tide which, while chaotic, can become a genuine experience of fraternity, a caravan of solidarity, a sacred pilgrimage" (*The Joy of the Gospel*, 87).

The baptism that John proclaimed is thus already beginning to be realized in the "mingling flood tide" of humanity that has appeared with him in the desert. Here we can see the promise of the gospel that Jesus will later embody: our deepest identity is to live in the reality of God's love where love of God is saturated with love of neighbor (Mark 12:30-31). To live in this wilderness of encounter is also to remain vulnerable to the heat, hunger, thirst, and fear that can overtake us and turn us against one another. In the first century, traveling together by caravan was essential for physical survival. So too for societal survival and relational flourishing in today's wider wilderness of encounter: it can be messy and chaotic, involving misunderstandings,

Can you think of a time when you recognized aspects of your identity flowing from your relationships with others or in service to your neighbor?

mistrust, discomfort, and setbacks. But when we persist in our desire to cling to one another in our diversity, we sometimes recognize glimpses of a new world being created.

[7]**And this is what he proclaimed: "One mightier than I is coming after me. I am not worthy to stoop and loosen the thongs of his sandals. [8]I have baptized you with water; he will baptize you with the holy Spirit."**

In John the Baptist's humble statement pointing away from himself and toward Christ, we find an implication that Jesus will have a baptizing ministry (v. 8). There is some question about whether Jesus himself baptized (see John 3:22 and 4:2, which seem to offer some contradiction). Whether or not Jesus baptized with water, John proclaims that Jesus will baptize with the Spirit (Matthew adds "and fire"; 3:11). Here John points to the distinction between his baptizing ministry and that of Jesus: God's activity and power are present and churning in a new way. The "holy wind" of the Spirit that breathed creation into birth (Gen 1:2; 2:7) is now present in the life of Christ. He will renew creation with his life breath and, as we will explore later in this volume, will immerse his followers in a new sacrificial way of life (Mark 10:38-40).

Just as John the Baptist was the gateway to Jesus' baptism and ministry, who are the people (family, mentors, saints) who led and loved you into baptism and discipleship?

[9]It happened in those days that Jesus came from Nazareth of Galilee and was baptized in the Jordan by John. [10]On coming up out of the water he saw the heavens being torn open and the Spirit, like a dove, descending upon him.

Liturgically, Christians celebrate Christ's baptism as an "epiphany" ("manifestation" or "theophany") of the love of our trinitarian God. The very Spirit that hovered over the waters at the dawn of creation flows through Jesus, who is God's creating and transforming love made incarnate in our time. In this passage, a classical style of biblical theophany is recalled as the heavens are "torn open," revealing God's presence in humanity.

Baptism is "incarnational," a sign of God's presence in humanity. What does this mean to you? How does this affect how you look at those who are baptized in Christ?

As Jesus emerges from the Jordan, the Spirit descends on him like a dove. Consider the resonance of this imagery with the dove that was a sign for Noah of the great flood's ending and the presence of dry land (Gen 8:8). Similarly, like the rainbow that appears to Noah as a sign of God's abiding relationship and love (Gen 9:13), Jesus enters into his post-baptismal ministry through the prism of heavens torn open. In solidarity with all of creation, Jesus recognizes that, though flooding and fear may persist (and indeed it will, beginning with Jesus' trek into the desert in verses 12-13), God's love is not the source of such tribulation, and is in fact deeper and stronger.

The imagery surrounding Jesus' baptism—and its reflection of the deeply personal, powerful experience of Jesus' relationship to Father and

How has your faith been a light for you, reflecting love of God, church community, or family? Would you call it a roaring fire, or a flickering but meaningful flame of love?

Spirit—holds meaning for our own baptisms. In the Christian tradition, the sacrament of baptism (literally "immersion") has also been called the sacrament of enlightenment (*Catechism of the Catholic Church*, 1216). Like the heavens torn open with blinding light, the baptized (especially those who are immersed), emerge from watery darkness into light. Even for adults and children baptized by a more modest sprinkling of water, baptism is followed with the liturgical giving of the light of Christ. Having *touched* God's love in Christ which swirls around us in baptism, we *see* God's love in a flickering candle, which for us holds the light of Christ's entire life and ministry.

Baptism is also called "christening"—and this word, too, holds in it the promise of both divine and human love. The word "Christ" reflects the Greek *christos* which, like the Hebrew-derived word *messiah*, means "anointed one." For parents and caregivers, to anoint is to touch with love. After bathing their children, parents will continue "hovering over" them, toweling them off and soothing them with oil. After an injury, a wound is cleansed and dressed with ointment. So too in baptism: the church continues to "hover over" the newly baptized, drying and anointing them with chrism oil. Even though there is no explicit anointing with oil in this baptismal scene with Jesus, the church has traditionally recognized that Christ was indeed anointed "with the Holy Spirit and power" (Acts 10:38).

Aside from the theophany of the Spirit descending upon Jesus in the form of a dove, we see that Jesus is himself a theophany of God's love. In the Jordan, Jesus enters into solidarity with those wilderness wanderers—that "chaotic flood tide" of humanity—hearing John's message and being baptized by him. And as Mark's gospel continues, Jesus will continue to companion unlikely associates: the unclean and uncouth (1:21-28, 40-45; 2:13-17; 5:1-20), women and children (7:24-30; 10:13-16; 14:3-9). To cherish our baptismal identity is to cherish that God's love for us is an incarnational love: Christ living in solidarity among us.

How has the presence of Christ in your baptized community "irrigated" the surrounding community through its prayer and acts of outreach and service?

11 **And a voice came from the heavens, "You are my beloved Son; with you I am well pleased."**

Just as the Spirit moves over the face of creation's waters (Gen 1:2) and God calls creation good (Gen 1:31), so too the Spirit descends upon

Jesus and he is called beloved and pleasing. Likewise, the combination of anointing and naming the anointed as "beloved" calls to mind the anointing of King David and the identification of him as the Lord's beloved son (Ps 2:7). Indeed, in the Bible, anointing is mentioned with regards to priests (Exod 28:41; Ps 133:2), prophets (Isa 61:1), and kings (1 Sam 15:1; Isa 45:1).

For Christians, Jesus is all three, but he is God's beloved in his unique nature: his particular way of being priest who sacrifices himself (Mark 10:38; Heb 7:27), prophet who speaks God's truth (Luke 4:18; Isa 61:1-2), and king who rules with loving justice (Matt 25:31-46). Jesus is Christ, anointed with the love of Father and Spirit. Deep within himself he is the presence of self-giving divinity. Christ, alive in God's love, is the very presence of God's self-giving love in our world.

How are you uniquely anointed with the touch of God's love? What is the imprint of God's life sealed deep within you, which shows itself in how you live?

In our own baptisms, we too are anointed or "sealed" with the Spirit, giving us the grace to be alive in God's creative, self-giving love. Well before the oil touches our heads, the bishop consecrated the oil, the sacred chrism, calling the Spirit into it with breath and ritual gesture. As baptized and anointed disciples, we continue to glisten with the same love that birthed our cosmos and took flesh in our humanity.

Our baptism is not simply a past event confined to photos or a baptismal register. Rather, it is a continuous proclamation that our deepest identity is not found in weariness or pain, pride or achievement, but in the reality that we are loved by God. When we hear ourselves proclaimed as God's beloved, we find ourselves alive in God's beloved: Jesus Christ.

Praying the Word / Sacred Reading

God of Glory,
All of creation shines with your presence and
        dazzling love.

We praise you for your loving energy,
a holy breath sweeping over water and earth,
forming and renewing mountains, glaciers,
        and seas.

In your wisdom,
you breathe this same powerful breath into all
        your children, woman and man.

You are source of glory in our humanity and
        holiness in our brokenness.

We know that your breath is always flowing
        through us,
a source of peace when we are anxious,
a source of holy dignity for our ordinary days,
a source of guidance along life's path.

Transforming God,
by the power of your Spirit, your holy breath,
enflame our hearts with love for all your
        people,

that our journeys might give life to the
journeys of others,
that our concern might be transformed into
justice for those who are oppressed,
that your Spirit might renew the face of the
earth.

Living the Word

- *Go on a pilgrimage (or, through web searching, an internet pilgrimage!) to the place of your baptism. Locate any pictures you may have from the day and talk to any people who may have been present, asking them what they remember. Take some time to imagine and journal about how your baptism unfolded.*
- *Make a "connections map" of those you are connected with in faith and service, including family, mentors, friends, co-workers, and people in your parish. Designate those connections that seem particularly strong, flowing with God's love. Be creative!*
- *Take time to immerse yourself in God's love by reconnecting with a loved one or friend and/or taking time in God's creation. How can you make this a regular practice?*

Alive in Christ's Life, Death, and Resurrection

Begin in quiet, asking God to assist you in your prayer and study. Then read the passage from Paul's letter to the Colossians, which encourages living in a way that repeats the pattern of Christ's death and resurrection.

Colossians 3:1-10, 12-16
1If then you were raised with Christ, seek what is above, where
Christ is seated at the right hand of God. 2Think of what is
above, not of what is on earth. 3For you have died, and your
life is hidden with Christ in God. 4When Christ your life ap-
pears, then you too will appear with him in glory.

5Put to death, then, the parts of you that are earthly: im-
morality, impurity, passion, evil desire, and the greed that is
idolatry. 6Because of these the wrath of God is coming [upon
the disobedient]. 7By these you too once conducted your-
selves, when you lived in that way. 8But now you must put
them all away: anger, fury, malice, slander, and obscene lan-
guage out of your mouths. 9Stop lying to one another, since
you have taken off the old self with its practices 10and have
put on the new self, which is being renewed, for knowledge,
in the image of its creator.

12Put on then, as God's chosen ones, holy and beloved,
heartfelt compassion, kindness, humility, gentleness, and pa-
tience, 13bearing with one another and forgiving one another,

if one has a grievance against another; as the Lord has forgiven you, so must you also do.
[14]And over all these put on love, that is, the bond of perfection. [15]And let the peace of Christ control your hearts, the peace into which you were also called in one body. And be thankful. [16]Let the word of Christ dwell in you richly, as in all wisdom you teach and admonish one another, singing psalms, hymns, and spiritual songs with gratitude in your hearts to God.

> *Following a few moments of quiet reflection on the passage from Colossians, consider the information provided in Setting the Scene. Continue using the questions in the margins for reflection or discussion.*

Setting the Scene

This passage from Colossians begins the letter's "paraenetic" or encouragement section and leads into what are commonly known as the "household codes" for ethical living. Selections from this passage are often used in worship on both Easter Sunday (vv. 1-4) and the Christmastime Feast of the Holy Family (vv. 12-17). As such, these verses offer us a useful and privileged way to reflect on our baptismal identity and how we live it in our daily lives.

Baptism in the Christian tradition picks up on both birth and death metaphors. On the one hand, baptism is birth into the Christian life, being born from above, of water and spirit (John 3:3-5). At the same time, as we see here, in baptism we have died and are raised with Christ. "[A]re you unaware," says Paul in a similar passage from Romans 6:3, "that we who were baptized into Christ Jesus were baptized into his death?" Baptism as birth and beginning is an idea that is as easy for us to embrace as it is to wrap our arms around the children we baptize. Baptism as death and resurrection, however, drowns us in mystery. We are tempted to limit its power to an appreciation of Christ's sacrifice for us, as though it were disconnected from our own identity, or to reflect on existence after physical death, beyond this lifetime. But here, imagery is used in a way that suggests our living here on earth, enlightened by Christ, is filled with dignity.

We are called to seek "what is above" (v. 1) knowing that in our baptisms we have already begun that movement into the light. We can honestly confront selfish and superficial attitudes inside of us, knowing that in baptism we have already stripped off the "old self." We engage in practices that, gradually, clothe us in compassion and self-giving, confident that we have been clothed in Christ.

When or how have you been challenged to ground your desire for God in your service and care for others?

Focus on smaller sections of the larger passage to deepen your appreciation of Paul's words.

Understanding the Scene Itself

[1]If then you were raised with Christ, seek what is above, where Christ is seated at the right hand of God. [2]Think of what is above, not of what is on earth. [3]For you have died, and your life is hidden with Christ in God. [4]When Christ your life appears, then you too will appear with him in glory.

Even in twenty-first-century democratic cultures, our imaginations come alive as we consume stories of medieval courts and contemporary royal intrigue, fantasy kingdoms, and ancient powers. In the face of first-century Roman power throughout the Mediterranean region and fed by biblical images of enthroned royalty in the line of David (e.g., 1 Kgs 2:12; Ps 89:4-5), we should not be surprised that early Christian hearers of this letter would be drawn to the image of Christ enthroned at the right hand of God (Matt 26:64; Heb 8:1).

The suffering and death of Jesus, the Christ, redefines kingship and royalty. How would you describe how the cross is more powerful than a crown?

As baptized disciples, we find our core identity in realities that are even deeper than the cosmic metaphor: Christ's kingship is a crucified one, his glory has already appeared in our lives, and we too share in Christ's crucified royal life—and are growing into it. Instead of finding ourselves perpetually outside the palace court, gawking at the power and pageantry as we look in, we see our destiny as enthroned in Christ's glory, where dignity is found in humility, and dying offers victory.

Having emerged from baptismal waters, we live in the light of Christ, where glory dwells more deeply than in what is typically glorified in our culture—the commercialization of beauty and sexuality, the cult of celebrity, the achievements of wealth or career. This Bible passage reminds us that our baptismal identity has gifted us with a great freedom: our real lives are already "hidden in Christ." In Christ, we see and experience dignity in what our culture tries to hide: chronic pain and terminal disease, disability and anxiety, hunger and poverty, addiction and depression. All of this has been touched by baptismal waters and, while the world may avert its gaze from humanity's fragility, in Christ it is a place of glory.

Indeed, it is the tender aspects of our humanity that allow us to be permeable to the "life of Christ" that washes over us in baptism. Our fragility is what opens us to the porous possibility already begun in baptism: that we are God's children now, and what we will be "has not yet been revealed" (1 John 3:2).

In what ways is human fragility a source of dignity or glory for you or someone close to you? How does fragility help us recognize our deepest selves or that of others?

When the fullness of our life in Christ appears in glory (v. 4), it will not grow from the surface-like veneer we often display. Rather, it will be the ultimate radiance of our deepest selves, whose illumination has already begun in baptism.

[5]Put to death, then, the parts of you that are earthly: immorality, impurity, passion, evil desire, and the greed that is idolatry. [6]Because of these the wrath of God is coming [upon the disobedient]. [7]By these you too once conducted yourselves, when you lived in that way. [8]But now you must put them all away: anger, fury, malice, slander, and obscene language out of your mouths. [9]Stop lying to one another, since you have taken off the old self with its practices [10]and have put on the new self, which is being renewed, for knowledge, in the image of its creator.

In these verses, we hear the call to "put to death" all immorality. Likewise, before approaching the waters of baptism, those to be baptized are asked (or, if they are children, their parents and godparents are asked) to first renounce sin, the glamour of evil, and indeed Satan, the father of sin and prince of darkness, with all his empty promises. Ritually, this may seem to be an insignificant moment, quickly passed through before the seemingly more joyous experiences of professing one's faith, the splashing of water, anointing with chrism, clothing with a white garment, and being given a lit candle. It is fairly normal to acclaim these later moments with song, laughter, and applause—but the renunciation of sin and Satan may seem like preliminary ritual jargon to get through before the main act.

And yet, to actively stand against the reality of sin in our world and in ourselves gets to the heart of Jesus' life and message. If we are tempted to think about Christ's sacrificial love (1 Cor 15:3; Rom 5:8) in a way that absolves us of any action on our part, our baptismal practice reflects the challenging truth that Jesus proclaimed a present and ongoing reign of God (Mark 1:15), calling the community of Jesus (in his time and ours) to "repent"—to literally *turn our lives around.* The beginning moments of the baptismal rite draw us into Jesus' call to continually turn away from self-centeredness and to live the reign of God that he preached and lived: a life of self-giving, serving, and sacrificing for others (Mark 10:43-45).

Where is the evidence that you have allowed your baptism to continue to grow in you, purifying your desires and actions? What signs do you see in your life?

Seen through the lens of the reign of God and our participation in it, baptism begins in us a lifelong process of purification, activated and sustained by God's grace in the life of Christ. God's grace flows through us to confront the reality of brokenness in our world. From this perspective, the reference to the "wrath of God" in verse 6 is a frank observation about the consequences of immorality and the stark need for our participation in the reign of God, rather than a divine act of punishment. In baptism, the reign of God begins to drown our self-centered desires so that they may die in us.

Our passage continues with an important exhortation to put away (i.e., to strip and take off) vices and fractious practices. Indeed, it has been the practice of many Christians to literally strip off their clothes before baptism. In the past,

How do you touch the world with intimacy and self-giving? What do you need to "take off" in order to do so?

adult baptisms were sometimes celebrated in enclosed baptisteries with those of the same gender. Today, modesty prevails, but we are still called to discard life's "clothing," to reject whatever restricts us from virtuous discipleship, to touch the grace that touches us, to love the world that is broken as we are broken. Our baptized bodies become a sign of not only the old that is passing away but also the new creation that lives and grows in us (2 Cor 5:17).

12 Put on then, as God's chosen ones, holy and
beloved, heartfelt compassion, kindness, humil-
ity, gentleness, and patience, 13 bearing with one
another and forgiving one another, if one has a
grievance against another; as the Lord has for-
given you, so must you also do. 14 And over all
these put on love, that is, the bond of perfection.
15 And let the peace of Christ control your hearts,
the peace into which you were also called in one
body. And be thankful. 16 Let the word of Christ
dwell in you richly, as in all wisdom you teach
and admonish one another, singing psalms,
hymns, and spiritual songs with gratitude in
your hearts to God.

In the Catholic baptismal liturgy, the clothing of the newly baptized infant or adult with a white garment is considered an "explanatory rite." It "explains" through ritual gesture what has already occurred in baptismal washing—that we have "put on Christ" and have been made a new creation. In the church's ministry, the white garment continues to be a powerful symbol of baptismal identity. Worn by liturgical ministers, it is especially obvious as the garment for altar servers but is also worn under the other liturgical garments of deacons, priests, and bishops. It is the garment for all the baptized and expresses our common dignity, deeper than any hierarchical status. And at our funerals, each of our caskets will be clothed with a white garment (the pall) as a final reminder of the ways in which we have been clothed in Christ throughout our lives and into death.

There is great comfort and joy in this ritual gesture and the image of being clothed (see Bar 5:1; Rom 13:14; Gal 3:27), but there is also a great challenge. Simply stated, to "put on Christ" is to be clothed and alive in the very life of Christ, to allow our lives to move and sway within the fabric and folds of Jesus' way of living. Here, this life is encapsulated with key virtues—compassion, kindness, humility, gentleness, and patience (v. 12)—all of which are lived most visibly in community. Indeed, it is only in community that baptized Christians are able to practice these virtues—in how we bear with, forgive, and sometimes even admonish one another.

Pick a virtue from verse 12 that is an important way you live your Christian life. How are you alive in that virtue?

Liturgy, where we dwell with the word of Christ and sing "psalms, hymns, and spiritual songs," becomes a sacred place to practice these virtues in a ritual way. By listening, singing, and praying together, we learn something about attentiveness, patience, and gentleness with one another. We can only live Christ's dying and rising *together*. And it is only in community that we can experience and live out the love of Christ—the "bond of perfection" that connects us with God and with each other. By living these virtues in community, we allow the reign of God to grow in our world.

How would you describe the Christian life as "clothing"? Is it structured and firm? Is it breathable? Does it sway?

At the same time, our baptismal living in community is always imperfect. Reflecting on what it means to be baptized, Cyril of Jerusalem reminds us that we are clothed in white, not because we have stopped sinning, but because we have been embraced as God's friends. We live *into* our white garments—indeed, we break them in—through a lifetime of conversion, urgently attentive to what needs to die in us, but also confident of the peace of Christ that has called us into this life and lives in our hearts (v. 15).

Praying the Word / Sacred Reading

Cross that leads us into glory,
Cross that bears a mystery:
Life outpoured and love exalted,
Tender grace that sets us free.

Grace that feeds us with affliction,
Bread of tears and saving cup.
A lifetime's thirst: to serve your people,
Bending down, you are raised up.

Stripped of all that is our bondage,
Drowning all that keeps us blind.
Life now clothed in light and freedom,
Robed in peace, alive in Christ.

Living the Word

- *As you continue to "live into" your white garments throughout your life, take advantage of opportunities to live virtue through service. Parishes and local agencies (e.g., homeless shelters, court-advocate programs, hospitals) often have great need for volunteers and mentors to make a meaningful difference in the community.*
- *Take time to balance your activity with spiritual practices like the Ignatian Examen, which is a way of paying attention to God's presence in daily life —understanding that God's light is present and active in the messy and the mundane for each of us. Search online or check with a local Jesuit retreat center for resources.*
- *Encountering Christ in the sacrament of reconciliation can also help us uncover our "turning away" from virtuous living and embrace our ongoing conversion—our "living into" the white garments of our baptism.*

Alive in Christian Community

Begin in quiet, asking God to assist you in your prayer and study. Then read the following passage from Ephesians that stresses the importance of community.

Ephesians 4:1-7, 11-13
1I, then, a prisoner for the Lord, urge you to live in a manner
worthy of the call you have received, 2with all humility and
gentleness, with pa-
tience, bearing with
one another through
love, 3striving to pre-
serve the unity of the
spirit through the bond
of peace: 4one body
and one Spirit, as you
were also called to the
one hope of your call;
5one Lord, one faith,
one baptism; 6one God and Father of all, who is over all and
through all and in all.

7But grace was given to each of us according to the measure
of Christ's gift.

11And he gave some as apostles, others as prophets, others
as evangelists, others as pastors and teachers, 12to equip the

holy ones for the work of ministry, for building up the body of Christ, [13]until we all attain to the unity of faith and knowledge of the Son of God, to mature manhood, to the extent of the full stature of Christ.

Following a few moments of quiet reflection on the passage from Paul to the Ephesians, consider the background information provided in Setting the Scene.

Setting the Scene

As with the Colossians passage we reflected on earlier, this selection from Ephesians begins the letter's "paraenetic" or encouragement section. The encouragement offered in this letter is especially focused on church unity and tells how, in living its unity, the church can live its mission in the world. Importantly, this letter does not simply address unity in one particular community but speaks of church unity in a more universal way. Indeed, it is likely that this letter was not only addressed to the Ephesians but to a wider network of diverse church communities being encouraged to live both diversity and unity.

In our time, this unity-in-diversity remains an important part of the church's mission in service to the world, and this passage from Ephesians will help us explore that mission as a key way in which we are alive in Christ. In a world that thrives on division, the common life of the Christian community (even and especially amid our differences) stands as a sacramental sign of unity.

Ephesians 4:1-7, 11-13 will be explored a few verses at a time to deepen your understanding.

Understanding the Scene Itself

[1]I, then, a prisoner for the Lord, urge you to live in a manner worthy of the call you have received,
[2]with all humility and gentleness, with patience, bearing with one another through love . . .

What does it mean to you to welcome or gather together as a Christian community?

When we approach the baptismal waters at church, the liturgy begins in the act of gathering at the church's doors, an image that may remind us of God's people gathering at the Jordan with John the Baptist. For adults preparing for baptism, this gathering at the threshold of the church usually occurs many months before baptism at the Rite of Acceptance in the Order of Catechumens. For infants, it happens on the same day as the baptism. In both cases, the priest or deacon asks for the name of the one to be baptized, and then *calls* and claims that person by name for Christ, gathering him or her into the church with the sign of the cross. Like the great prophets, the soon-to-be-baptized person is called by name as he or she stands at the threshold of new life and mission (Exod 3:4; 1 Sam 3:4).

While this liturgical gathering provides a wonderful ritual image, there is concern today about what seems to be happening to those gathered and "called by name" in these ritual moments. Record numbers of Catholics (and other Christians) are no longer attending Mass or participating in parish life on a regular basis. Is this lack of participation "worthy of the call" that has been received, what Vatican II identified as a *universal call to holiness* for all who have been baptized?

In addressing this question, it may be helpful to consider what it means to "live in a manner worthy of the call." The Greek word *peripateō* is translated here as *live*. More literally, it means to *walk* on the path of this call or vocation. We might call to mind the "way of Wisdom" described in the Old Testament (Prov 4:11) or early references to the Christian movement as "the Way" (Acts 9:2). Pope Francis also uses the image of a "path of holiness" to describe the ways in which all the baptized, already graced in baptism, are walking into fruitful holiness even when it may not be obvious to them or others (*Rejoice and Be Glad*, 15–16). Francis

Call to mind those you know who are baptized but disconnected from a faith community. How are they nevertheless living a Christian calling?

notes that holiness grows through "small gestures," sacrifices, and steps in daily life—putting a stop to gossiping, using a last ounce of energy to listen to one's children, taking a moment for prayer or for a poor person on the street. Francis's examples are excellent illustrations of the baptismal virtues highlighted in the Ephesians passage: humility, gentleness, patience, bearing with one another—virtues that can point to particular ways baptized Christians live their mission in the world.

What are the "small steps" you have taken to grow in virtue? What have you learned about yourself and how the grace of God is present in you?

While we as a church should never be complacent about missing members, we can find joy in observing and nurturing the goodness of the baptized, both in the church and in the world. Indeed, coming together at the threshold of the church before baptism is just such an opportunity as we reverence God's presence and activity in all those who mingle there—in the almost-baptized infants, cradle Catholics, journeying adult catechumens, weekly parishioners, and visiting family members who may only be occasional worshipers. So too are many other "threshold moments" outside liturgy when the parish is in contact with a larger community of service, neighborhood, and civic engagement. This way of looking at our baptismal identity respects the ongoing walk of the entire Body of Christ, responding to the call of mutual gathering and opening up future pathways along the way of holiness.

. . . [3]striving to preserve the unity of the spirit through the bond of peace: [4]one body and one Spirit, as you were also called to the one hope of your call; [5]one Lord, one faith, one baptism; [6]one God and Father of all, who is over all and through all and in all.

Where have you seen examples of a Christian community showing love for one another?

One of the "calling cards" of the early Christian community was recorded by Tertullian, an early Christian theologian, who wrote that those outside the community would say of Christians: "See how they love one another." This observation was a realization of Jesus' hope for his community of disciples: that others would know of their common discipleship in their love for one another (John 13:35).

Unfortunately, although we still sing the words "they'll know we are Christians by our love," the truth is that contemporary church life, in Catholicism and beyond, may seem more marked by division, conflict, and polarization than love. And yet the early Christian witness and these words from Ephesians reject all factionalism with a confidence that the "one Spirit" is able to robustly move through various disagreements and divisions, as it has since the early church (see Acts 10; 15:1-29; Gal 2:1-11). Even in the midst of difference and debate, there is a strong sense of identity here as "one body" that is united in seven creedal touchstones (one body, Spirit, hope, Lord, faith, baptism, and God

Are there types of church division that cause you pain? Consider why they are painful for you. How do you deal with these feelings? What gives you hope?

the Father of all). Embracing a creed is not so much about intellectual assent as giving one's heart to something; our common baptismal belonging is deeper than our minds, reaching to the very core of who we are. Thus the letter to the Ephesians prefaces a list of diversity in the church (vv. 11-12) by providing a list of commitments (vv. 4-6), uniting us deeply—at the level of the heart—with God and with one another.

In the early church, the importance of "one baptism" flowed from the experience of Pentecost (Acts 2:2-4) which unleashed an outward, centrifugal force, allowing the life of Jesus to be spoken *into* various languages and cultures, as well as an inward, centripetal force, *gathering* many numbers into one baptized community (2:38). The subsequent history of the Christian movement is dizzying in its cultural breadth and expression. Having been gathered into "one Lord, one faith, one baptism," we have been given the gift of Christ, who is simultaneously present in all cultural expressions of his life, and transcendent over all these distinct ways of being alive in Christ. We are at the same time unique and united. This is the work of the "one Spirit."

Indeed, in the church's diverse peoples and cultures, as well as in the rich ecumenical movement that has developed in the past century, we can discern the "unity of Spirit" that is the source of what we recognize as our shared "one baptism." Vatican II's *Decree on Ecumenism* called baptism a "sacramental bond of unity" linking all who have been reborn in it and stated that all who have been baptized (whether in the Catholic Church or not) are incorporated together into Christ (22). What is true in our approach to ecumenism is also true in how we view baptism in general: it makes us members of "one another" (see Eph 4:25; *CCC*, 1267). As in the early church, conflict and debate can be the means through which our baptismal belonging to one another is deepened. It is slow work, but we can be encouraged that it is the work of the one Spirit into which we have all been baptized.

Have you experienced times when faith communities have grown through conflict, even though it was difficult?

Ultimately, the "unity of the Spirit" experienced by those baptized in the name of Father, Son, and Spirit is a challenging witness to the wider culture, as well as to the baptized themselves who are steeped in that culture. The Spirit who is called down upon the waters of baptism immerses all it touches in a lifelong yearning for unity—one already present in baptism but also stretching toward the future, even beyond our lifetimes. This is the same Spirit that flows between Father and Son with a strength that is both intimate and infinite—so infinite that it invites us and all of creation into that love and life. This infinite longing for communion flows into us in baptism and is a gift and lifelong

"See how they love one another."

vocation, that the world might see a community alive in an ever-present and slowly-deepening unity.

[7]But grace was given to each of us according to the measure of Christ's gift.

[11]And he gave some as apostles, others as prophets, others as evangelists, others as pastors and teachers, [12]to equip the holy ones for the work of ministry, for building up the body of Christ, [13]until we all attain to the unity of faith and knowledge of the Son of God, to mature manhood, to the extent of the full stature of Christ.

We have explored two key challenges facing today's church community: the disconnection many feel with the church, as well as the divisions apparent within the church. This passage from Ephesians offers encouragement in the midst of both realities, helping us embrace our baptismal identity and life in Christ. These final verses of the passage provide a "nuts-and-bolts" approach to building up the body of Christ. The church helps its baptized members to experience being "alive in Christ" when it effectively nurtures and draws upon the gifts of each

member. One of the key achievements of the Second Vatican Council is that it has helped Catholics embrace the understanding that through baptism all members of Christ are called to ministry. The baptized themselves are the "living stones," built upon Christ the cornerstone, who make up the household of God (Eph 2:19-20; 1 Pet 2:4-5).

How are you a "living stone" building up the community? Where do you see the need for your particular form of ministry, activity, or leadership?

We are still living into this vision and, to be frank, we often pay too little attention to how essential each of us is as a living stone, and how the "structural integrity" of our community household suffers when "precious stones" are missing or not utilized. To put it another way, as church community we are often content to build up only some areas of the household that is the church, while allowing a pile of living stones to sit unused on the work lot. These are stones that have been kilned by a loving creator, holding within them the potential to strengthen, beautify, and expand our community and its mission. The key to the church's revitalization can be found in the individual callings and giftedness of each of its members.

The wisdom offered in Ephesians is open-ended, and the various types of leadership named in verse 11 are simply a starting point (see also 1 Cor 12). Biblical scholars suggest that in this list, the naming of apostles and prophets is meant to show the church's past foundation, while the inclusion of evangelists, pastors, and teachers reflects later gifts and leadership roles (including those in today's community). As followers of the risen Christ, we have been baptized into a body that stretches back across time, a story of continued growth into the "full stature of Christ." From its first decades, our community has experienced the Spirit at work through the efforts of various leaders (sometimes with very different visions) building upon one another (see Acts 18:24-27; 1 Cor 1:12; 3:4-22). God's fruitful activity is present amid collaboration: no matter who does the planting and watering, God gives the growth (1 Cor 3:6-7).

How has your understanding of baptism deepened or expanded through your reflection on these passages?

The growth nurtured by our loving God is the life of Christ flowing into our world through the Spirit and experienced sacramentally in baptism. Baptism is an ongoing spring of living water welling up in each of us (John 4:14), that we might in turn be sources of growth for the community and for the reign of God. As a community, we grow slowly into the maturity of Christ's life, death, and resurrection. Immersed in that community and bathed in God's love, together we are alive in Christ.

Praying the Word / Sacred Reading

Ever-loving God,
You are present to us at all times and in all
seasons.
We see You in the morning light that breaks
into our dreaming.
We hear You in the music of rainstorm and
birdsong.
We feel You in the stirring wind that rustles
the leaves and rattles our bones.

Fire of Love,
You who called the world into being,
Have also called us together.
In Your continuing work of creation,
Walk with us and be our Strength.

Fill us with Your Presence that we might be
Comfort, hope, and peace for each other.
Enable us to be Your Love to one another.

Empower us to bring that Love to the world.

(Co-written with Julia Jones Huyck)

Living the Word

- *Take time to explore faith practices that you are not familiar with or are even skeptical about, perhaps making time to visit local churches beyond your tradition or denomination to experience their worship style, or join them for service opportunities. What similarities or new ways of experiencing God's presence do you observe through participation?*

- *Spend some time discerning or reflecting upon your own personal strengths, gifts, charisms, or personality. How is God specifically calling you to be active in your parish and community? What gifts do you have to share? You may wish to seek the help of a spiritual director, a parish leader, or various resources available for discerning personal gifts and charisms.*